This Book Belongs To:

....

....

....

THE

FEMINIST:

What Feminism Is Really About, Breaking The Glass Ceiling & Ending Misogyny And Sexism

TABLE OF CONTENTS

INTRODUCTION

Feminism, also known as gender equality is an ever-progressive, social motion that has confronted the long-status gender inequity. It is one of the 17 sustainable development goals (SDG) by the United Nations.

Feminism means different things to different people. To some, it means freedom and acceptance of all individuals regardless of color, gender or background. It means equal treatment for everyone, irrespective of their gender, race, ethnicity, age, etc. For others, feminism involves feminists, women who can't be feminine and wish to displace men in every sector of the society. Some others view feminism as a man-hating scheme or as a medium to end patriarchy. The meanings are non-exhaustive!

For centuries, women all around the world have been oppressed and denied fundamental rights. They have been told that their value lay in their looks and virginity, and nothing else. They have been told not to be as independent, bold, ambitious, and purposeful as men. They have been underpaid compared to men and they have been denied representation in leadership roles. Gender discrimination does not only limit careers but also ruins lives in the most unfair and inhumane ways. It is even so heart-breaking to mention that some feminist moves are met with brutal violence.

Know that feminism seeks equality, acceptance, justice, and to end damage towards all people, especially to women. It aims at taking down gender inequality and the systems that uphold it. These inequalities include pay inequality, gender-based inaccessibility to education and health care, gender-based violence, etc.

It advocates for a society that does not relate any ability, activity or clothes with any gender. Feminism started as a drive striving for gender equality by resisting patriarchal attitude and traditions that abuse and subordinate women. Feminism is good. Feminism is what we need today. It exists to improve and defend the rights of women and girls all over the world. Gender equality is its single most important goal.

When women and girls have the materials and opportunities they need to excel, it's a win for everyone, everywhere. In spite of the progress towards gender equality, though slow and uneven, inequality still continues.

There will be no peace among the genders, among the races, among individuals until we create it in our very own hearts. Feminism not only fights against the inequality in the society, but also the voices that tell us that feminism is no longer necessary, that it no longer has a place in today's world. Ending gender inequality is everybody's business. Feminism is the tool to break the glass ceiling.

CHAPTER ONE:

WHAT FEMINISM IS REALLY ABOUT

WHAT IS FEMINISM?

Feminism has gazillion definitions subject to who you ask. It is practically the notion that men and women should have equal privileges, entitlements, treatment and opportunities, and not necessarily equality in gender roles or bodily capabilities of both sexes.

It is a significant concept that strives for social, political, economic, cultural and all the different rights of women being equal to those of men. It prioritizes the need for all women to have equal opportunities in life - fair employment and wages, ownership of assets, education, legal and marital rights. For so long, women have been disregarded and withheld opportunities. Feminism exists to end these systems of inequality and discrimination.

Feminism implies that all genders have the same rights and opportunities. It`s about valuing various women's strengths and identities, and striving to empower all women to enjoy their full rights. It ensures that girls and women enjoy equal life opportunities that boys and men also enjoy.

Gender discrimination downplays the very existence of our social shape and diminishes the human potential. It denies about half of the population worldwide the chance to live their lives. No one has to be denied fundamental rights – right to vote, to maintain political office, to be educated, to own assets due to their gender.

Prioritizing gender equality and feminism therefore assist all people around the world.

Today, thanks to feminism, gender-based abuse, violence, harassment, and discrimination are extensively addressed and as such, women are protected from them. This is what feminism is supposed to be.

WHAT FEMINISM IS SUPPOSED TO BE

Feminism is supposed to advocate for the social, economic and political equality of all genders, with primary attention on addressing the inequalities and injustices that women and girls face and promoting their rights and opportunities.

Feminism also informs the public about the ordeals of women all over the world to make sure that all voices and identities are included in the fight for equality.

Overall, feminism seeks a society where everyone enjoys equal rights and opportunities, no matter the gender. It prioritizes cooperation and peace, instead of conflict and hatred.

WHAT FEMINISM IS NOT SUPPOSED TO BE

Feminism is not supposed to advocate the idea that women are better than men. It's not supposed to prohibit men from dialogues about gender equality. It is not a movement that marginalizes the rights and opportunities of people based on their race, color, class or gender. Feminism also is not meant to be anti-male.

WHO IS A FEMINIST?

You are a feminist if you believe in and advocate for gender equality for women and all people everywhere.

WHAT DO FEMINISTS DO?

Feminists engage in diverse activities geared toward addressing issues women and girls face such as inequalities, discrimination, violence and injustices. They also create awareness about gender equality.

Additionally, they advocate for women's rights with regards to education, healthcare, employment, wage pay, leadership roles, political roles, etc. They conduct campaigns, protests and contribute to policy-making to make sure that the society is equitable for everyone, especially women.

CAN ANYONE BE A FEMINIST?

Of course! If you believe in gender equality, then you're a feminist. It's not about one gender being better than the other. No! It's about getting to know how inequality affects all genders, both men and women alike. Feminism recognizes gender-based discrimination and ensures that everyone enjoys their full rights, regardless of gender, race or whatsoever.

WE SHOULD ALL BE FEMINISTS

Gender equality is a fundamental human right. We all ought to believe in it. When no gender, race or religion is held to precise requirements, all of us benefit. We must all trust this essential concept of gender equality, and as a result of this, we should all be feminists.

CHAPTER TWO:

ARE YOU A FEMINIST?

Ask yourself these questions and answer them candidly to know where you stand on feminism:

1. Do you agree that men and women should have equal rights, opportunities and treatment? If not, why? What are you afraid of if equality is achieved?

2. Do you believe it is fair to offer women partial rights as compared to men who enjoy complete array of different rights and opportunities?

3. Do you agree that only a sect of people should enjoy certain opportunities and rights? If not, why?

4. What's the origin of your beliefs about feminism?

5. Do your beliefs feel right for you? Do they align with who you truly are — honest, integrity-filled, compassionate, and fair or otherwise?

6. Do you agree that a society that hinders certain individuals from having access to complete rights would prosper?

7. If you consider equality for all, are you capable of taking a courageous stand for it, in a manner that feels proper to you, for your very own lifestyles and for your very own sphere of influence?

CHAPTER THREE:

15 QUALITIES EVERY FEMINIST SHOULD POSSESS

Belief In Equality

We believe in and advocate for equal rights, opportunities and privileges for everyone all around the world, most especially women.

Question Traditions

We question old traditions and also advocate for the right to choose. You don't have to be a housewife if you don't want to. Additionally, we advocate for shared domestic work as one partner's time is not more important than the other partner. We also teach our kids how to appreciate and respect the other gender instead of being fearful or intimidated by them.

Know our Self Worth

We know our self-worth and value. Therefore, we refuse to be thrown into submission and oppression.

Advocate for Female Leadership

We advocate for female representation in places of decision-making.

Advocate for Equal Pay

We advocate for fair and equal pay for both men and women for the same work.

Self-awareness

We, feminists are aware of our strengths, weaknesses, opportunities and threats.

True to Yourself

Stay completely true to yourself. Be comfortable in your own skin! Be proud of yourself and your accomplishments. Never ever change who you are in order to please someone else.

Self-care and being concerned for others

We always look after our physical, spiritual and emotional well-being, as well as care for and support others to do the same.

Dismantling bias

We know that society doesn't offer certain people certain privileges because of their gender, race or class. It is up to us to expose this discrimination when we encounter them and urge the people around us to do the same. Most importantly, our won conduct must be void of harassment and inequality.

Collaboration

We seek to build a platform to get everyone on board so that they can be equally heard and respected. We also work in unison to achieve our goals. We make clear decisions that align with our goals and purpose. We voice out our beliefs and set the record straight.

Courage

Courage is like a driving force that makes us stand up for what we believe in and take risks. We need courage in order to face our fears head on and not shy away from them. We, feminists are outspoken in advocating for our beliefs.

Confidence

Confidence is super important because it helps us believe in our abilities and make decisions without doubting ourselves. Confidence also boosts productivity.

Optimistic

We need optimism to maintain a positive mindset, especially in difficult times. We need optimism in order to see failures as opportunities for growth and improvement. Allow your optimism to rub off on others.

Not scared to Stand Up for What You Believe In

When we see something wrong in the society, we do not stay mute but stand up for what is right and take action. We, feminists are not ashamed to declare who we are and what we believe in.

Not bothered by what people say or think about you

People are always going to talk. Haters are always going to hate. What they say isn't going to define you but you get to define you.

5 THINGS YOU SHOULDN'T BE ASHAMED OF AS A FEMINIST

Just because you practice some actions doesn't mean you're a 'bad' feminist and shouldn't make you feel like you don't deserve to be called a feminist. Here are five things you shouldn't be ashamed of as a feminist:

Liking Pink

One significant feature of a feminist is being true to who you are. Whether you like pink or black, like make-up or not, prefer heels to flats or dresses to jeans, always stay true to yourself and appreciate yourself.

Caring About Your Looks

We, feminists are allowed to care about how we look. After all, how you dress is how you'll be addressed.

Feeling Vulnerable

It's OK to feel tired, helpless or dependent sometimes. This doesn't make you a bad feminist. It's also OK to need help from men when it comes to picking up a heavy package or navigating through something.

Daydreaming About Family

Daydreaming about your wedding day or beautiful moments you'll create with the love of your life or the number of kids you want to have and so on doesn't mean you're a bad feminist. Feminism advocates for choice. It allows you to walk down any path that makes you happy.

Traditions

Having faith in God doesn't make you a bad feminist. Some traditions have been hurtful to women while some have emphasized the values women bring to society. Celebrating these traditions doesn't mean you're a bad feminist.

WHY IS BEING FEMININE IMPORTANT?

Why not? Women are unquestionably beautiful on the inside and out. To begin, femininity is appealing. This is why so many people initially gravitate toward women. You'll get attention and make heads turn. When you are feminine, you feel good about yourself, which boosts your self-esteem and confidence. Additionally, the feminine aura exudes kindness and warmth. It simplifies life. You need to figure out the best way to embrace your femininity in a way that helps you achieve your goals of happiness in life and even love. Some people say that makeup is what defines femininity, while others say that clothes are all that matter.

Even though makeup or clothes is a good start, being feminine is more than that. Your physical appearance, your actions, and your feelings all contribute to your feminine aura. Appreciating your body and releasing its inherent power to brighten the world are also aspects of femininity.

Another common reason women choose to appear more feminine is to start a relationship. They want to be attractive with their partners.

HOW TO EMBRACE AND KEY INTO YOUR FEMININITY

Being feminine is a balance of cultural, social, and biological characteristics as well as attributes and behaviors that define women. A way of thinking, a way of life, and a set of beliefs are all aspects of femininity. Also, it's a way of doing things and a style. All of these factors contribute to a woman's beauty.

Femininity is not a flaw or a reason to think you are less significant than a man, contrary to popular belief. In fact, being feminine entails appreciating all of the beautiful qualities that women possess, such as intelligence, grace, beauty, empathy, and so forth.

In general, women who identify as feminine value relationships and care for others. Don't worry if you think being feminine is something you just weren't born with. The good news is that you can learn to be more feminine in a way that comes easily to you. Here are tips on how to key into your femininity:

1. Feminine looks

- ❖ Style your hair. To look good, take some time to work on your hair. Try arranging your hair with hair clips or using a curling iron to make spiraling love locks. Grow your hair. Long hair is widely regarded as feminine. If you prefer short hair, you don't have to give up on being feminine.
- ❖ Put some makeup on. Use soft pinks or reds on your lips.Just minimal make-up that makes you feel good.
- ❖ Do your eyebrows. They shape the face, frame the eyes, and literally frame the female face. Don't let your eyebrows get too bushy.

❖ Put on pretty shoes. Women know that no outfit is complete without the right shoes. Heels, in particular, give the impression of being feminine.

❖ Take care of your face to bring out its beauty. You will feel amazing after a gentle facial massage and a thorough cleansing of your face.

❖ Apply moisture to your skin. Fundamental to femininity is healthy, soft skin. So that others are drawn to your smooth skin, select lotions and creams that both prevent and repair damage.

❖ Wear jewelry because it sends a message of elegance. Even minimal jewelry makes your eyes and smile stand out.

❖ A little manicure can do a lot of good. If your nails are chipped or bitten, you going to look far from feminine. Make an effort to maintain good nail shape. Pink or nude nail colors give off a sophisticated vibe and keep your hands looking great all the time.

❖

2. Choose clothing that emphasizes your best features and flatters your female body shape.

Basically, you shouldn't cover your body with baggy clothes all the time. This doesn't mean you have to wear tight too - just clothes that fit your body well. Dress in a way that emphasizes your curves and gives you confidence in your appearance.

Choose a sweet color the next time you shop for clothes. Select a fit that emphasizes your body's curves and shape. Add a belt to give them shape and wear them with skirts, jeans, etc.

A boa or scarf instantly adds a feminine touch to an outfit. These accessories draw attention to your face and add an additional layer of mystery to your appearance.

Red conveys your feminine qualities, whether on a blouse, dress, or lipstick. Red is associated with vivacity and passion in our minds, and if you allow

yourself to express your inner power through color,
your femininity will soar. Allow the colors to captivate.

For a pretty and delicate look, you can choose bright
and classy colors like lavender, baby blue, butter
yellow, soft pink, or a muted mauve. You can choose
neutral colors like gray, black, and brown.

3. Wear perfume

Choose a scent that excites you while remaining subtle.
The right fragrance keeps you on top of your body.
Scent is typically closely associated with memory.

4. Maintain good posture

Sit straight, cross your legs at the ankles, and keep
your chin up and shoulders back. Also, keep a straight
face. Everyone looks good with a straight posture and
shoulders that are aligned. You will instantly improve
your appearance if you maintain good posture.

5. Limit swearing and vulgarity

Violent language and jokes are far from being feminine. Being feminine requires you to be more creative and clever with your words. Try using phrases like "Good lord!" the next time you are infuriated. Keep the F word from being used in inappropriate contexts.

6. Be confident

Confidence is the foundation of a powerful woman. You can be confident in the following ways:

- Concentrate on your accomplishments and strengths.
- Keep a list of your top five qualities and use them whenever you need a boost.
- Wear clothes that highlight who you are to exude confidence and beauty.
- Be around positive people that inspire you to become your best.
- Stay away from the people who cut you down.

- Accept your beauty, skill, and most importantly, your value.
- Accept compliments with graciousness and refrain from self-pitying.

Women who are self-assured are aware of their life's objectives and are unwilling to wait for men to fulfill their dreams. Additionally, they are proud of their strengths.

Women don't need the attention and approval of others to feel good, so not insisting on excess makeup is a sign of personal confidence. Women who apply a lot of makeup may give the impression that they are shallow.

7. Show empathy

Placing yourself in people's shoes and experiencing life through their eyes is an essential feminine trait. When you express your concern for others, you will bring attention to your feminine qualities.

8. Discrete

The feminine side is somewhat private and reserved. Refrain from revealing too much about yourself right away. Be helpful and kind to those around you while you wait for your turn to speak. Be courteous when conversing with others.

You can support a pleasant and invigorating discussion with good judgment. It demonstrates that you are not afraid to express your thoughts.

9. Be graceful

Although there is no one right way to act gracefully, here are some ways to appear graceful:

- Add a subtle touch to your swing by walking softly and swaying your hips.
- Take slow, steady steps.
- Don't fiddle with your clothes or clench your fists.
- The best way to make yourself appear approachable is to keep your body still and relaxed.
- By choosing to speak more gracefully, you can show off your femininity through your words.

When speaking, make gentle, natural hand gestures. Being feminine means paying attention to your heart and mind, as well as speaking your mind.

- Dance helps you maintain a connection between your body and your spirit by moving to music. Use your feminine power by simply experiencing movement in your female body.

10. Vulnerability

Far too many women mistake feminine strength for refusing to rely on others. You ought to concede when you can't follow through with something or need assistance here and there.

11. Tune with nature

Femininity is about giving life to everything around you. Grow plants, rear pets and so on. Enhancing the beauty of your surroundings will strengthen your connection to your femininity.

12. Take some time to reflect on your feelings, aspirations, and life.

You will align your femininity with a sense of purpose as you learn more about your motivations and goals. If you've had a long day, indulge in some self-care by reading a good book, taking care of your skin, or relaxing with some music to let the stress leave your body. For a well-deserved night's sleep, treat yourself to spa treatments at home and spend a little extra on comfortable sleep gear. After all, you should do whatever makes you feel good!

Love yourself constantly. Only you can make yourself feel powerful and beautiful. Therefore, just be you, realize that you are sufficient, and express yourself.

13. Help other people understand their emotions

A lot of people don't know how to identify or process their emotions. You can help a friend or family member get through a hard time. Engage them in conversations too.

14. Recognize your partner's contributions

Your husband or boyfriend would like to hear you express your gratitude for his contributions. By showing appreciation, you show your partner how much you value them and that you rely on them.

15. Be hygienic

Hygiene and femininity go hand in hand. Make time to groom yourself. You'll feel better the more you take care of yourself. Take care of our hair and skin as well as maintaining a healthy mind and body. It is essential.

16. Be charming

Play along with non-offensive jokes and have a good time. Build a good sense of humor.

17. Have a positive mindset

When things fall apart, still believe that there is light at the end of the tunnel. Believe that your greatest achievements are already within you. People will begin to perceive you as more confident as a result of your positive attitude.

18. Spend time with your girls

A girl's day out is a fantastic opportunity to relax, have fun, and feel great! Encourage other women. As you interact with other people, let your strength and resilience shine through. Let go of judgment and criticism and allow yourself to be supported and loved.

19. Forgive

Forgiveness necessitates letting go of resentment and anger. You stop expecting others to be perfect when you accept them as they are. That also applies to you.

You can let go of the need to always be right by being forgiving. It can give you power because it demonstrates strength and vulnerability.

20. Take care of your mental health

Even though we tend to put a lot of emphasis on our physical health, we shouldn't neglect our mental health. It's easier to let go of negative feelings and thoughts when you have a healthy mind.

You'll be able to walk taller, smile more, and hold your head up high. Therefore, whenever it's necessary, grant yourself permission to solely concentrate on your happiness. In the end, being feminine begins within and spreads outward.

21. Give compliments

Compliments are a great way to show your affection. Gratify anyone for anything, from their attire to their accomplishments. Tell someone when you notice something about them that you really like or admire!

Be sincere and specific at the same time. False compliments, after all, only make other people feel uncomfortable.

22. Be careful with your words

With the right words, you'll sound more like the woman you want to be. Choose your words carefully. Be courteous whenever possible. Be appreciative of the assistance you receive. Having good manners exemplifies elegance and femininity.

23. Accept compliments and gifts

Don't dismiss a compliment or gift out of modesty; instead, accept it. Learn to respond with a heartfelt "thank you" when you are praised for your kind and gracious nature. You'll come across as gentler and more understanding when you appreciate and accept these things.

24. Self-esteem

Stop constantly seeking validation. Instead, work on building your self-esteem and taking pride in who you are. You will be able to stop relying on others' approval because of this. Do things that make you feel good and happy inside and out. Engage with positive and encouraging people as well.

25. Support your partner

Offer to assist him whenever he requires it and help him around. Offer to assist your partner if they are having difficulty with a project. Keep in mind that the smallest details matter. Throughout his highs and lows, be by his side and encourage him when he needs it. Be the additional impetus he requires to improve his life. Being feminine means showing your man compassion when he needs it the most.

26. Communication

Communicate better. Beyond merely responding with a "yes" or "no," asking questions fosters a deeper conversation and strengthens relationships.

Listen too. It shows that you care when you agree with everything someone says.

27. Modesty

Do you ever find yourself talking about your entire life to someone? If that's the case, you might want to be careful.

CHAPTER FOUR:

REASONS PEOPLE HATE FEMINISM, FEMINISTS AND THE FEMINIST'S MOVEMENT

There are many people out there that believe in equal rights and opportunities for all genders but desist from calling themselves feminists. For those people who are nevertheless hiding and cautious to publicly embody their feminist beliefs due to the stigma related to the motion, it's okay. Be pleased with your zeal for equality and change. Never let the lack of knowledge of others dilute your passion for feminism.

Here are a couple of reasons people hate feminism, feminists and the feminist's movement:

1. Feminism has been related to strong and aggressive women. Some people worry that feminism will result in terrible shifts in relationships, society, culture, power and business.

2. Some people worry that feminists will dominate and control men.

3. Some people worry that feminism will displace men in the world of influence, impact, authority, and financial possibilities.

4. Some people worry that feminism will overturn traditions and certain gender roles, and they think it is horrifying and wrong.

5. They don't identify as feminists because they assume it is very victimizing.

6. Some others don't identify as feminists because they have never experienced violence or inequality.

7. There are people who think feminism makes no sense.

In the end, all of us ought to honor the values and beliefs that sense proper and desirable to us.

CHAPTER FIVE:

THE GOOD, THE BAD AND THE UGLY - MISCONCEPTIONS ABOUT FEMINISM

Illusions surrounding feminism exist to confuse people who don`t absolutely get the picture of what it entails. Ignorance is the engine that births these misconceptions, stigmatization, opposition and hate towards feminism and feminists. These misconceptions include the following:

Myth 1: Feminism is a fight for women to have power over men

Feminism is about doing away with biased forces that favor only a few people and mar people of all genders. It's not about one gender better than another.

It seeks equality, acceptance, justice, and to end damage towards all people. It attempts to stabilize the power struggle among genders. It isn't about getting rid of power from anyone or making one gender superior to the other.

Women lack plenty of fundamental human rights that permit them to have autonomy over their own bodies and lives. Giving them their human rights does not give them power over men.

Myth 2: Feminism is a westernized idea

Feminism is not restricted to Western countries. It`s a worldwide motion that seeks for equal treatment for everyone, irrespective of their gender, race, ethnicity, age, etc. Even though patriarchy dominates majority of countries, feminism actually applies to all societies, anywhere and everywhere.

Myth 3: Feminism is about hating men

No. That's not true. This myth stemmed from the fact that men are often the ones who oppose the idea of feminism. Even though men had been oppressing women for years, we feminists do not hate men. All we need is to be treated as their equals and with respect. Feminism is not about female superiority, but equality among genders.

Myth 4: Feminists can only be women

A lot of people think feminism is a woman's issue that they do not want to be involved in because it is closely related to the word femininity. That's just plain ignorance! Feminism has no prejudice or bias. It calls on all and sundry to advocate for gender equality in the society. Men can be feminists too and it doesn't make them less of who they are.

Myth 5: Feminism is dangerous to men

Not at all! Feminism strives for gender equality perhaps to alleviate men of their roles as breadwinners and the burdens around such roles that harm them emotionally, mentally, and physically. Feminism seeks financial independence for women.

Myth 6: All feminists are the same

Presuming that all feminists act and think the same is a misconception. Feminists are not all the same as feminism is unique to each and every single person on the planet.

It comes from personal experiences of different people. Although feminists do have common objectives, they are not all the same. It includes liberal feminism, socialist feminism, radical feminism, and inter-sectional feminism, each with its own views and priorities.

Myth 7: Feminists don't joke, are angry and bitter all of the time

Feminism is not about anger and bitterness. Women are nonetheless regarded as bad moms if they prioritize their careers. How can someone not be upset about the violence and the discrimination that has gone on for years without redress? So yes, we're on occasion aggressive and bitter but the feminist motion is about acceptance and justice. Rather than being irritated and hateful in the direction of others, we ought to advocate for equality, end this vicious cycle of discrimination, and empower those around us. Women should be able to choose their ambitions without pressures from anywhere.

Myth 8: Feminists cannot be feminine

Feminism isn't practically about being feminine or masculine. It is about having the right to choose and express yourself in whatever way you choose, without being limited by societal expectations. It is all about choice and freedom. Feminists can choose to be feminine or not, wear make-up or not, wear what they want and behave in whatever way they wish. Feminism does not undermine femininity. Instead, it enables people to discover new things and ideas.

Myth 9: Feminism underrates culture and traditional roles

Assuming that feminists hate culture and traditional roles is a misconception. Feminism is about giving people the liberty to pursue the jobs and careers that they want without being constrained by gender stereotypes.

Myth 10: Feminism is no longer integral

The rise in gender-based violence and discrimination against women demonstrates that the fight for gender equality is more crucial today than ever before.

While there may be a multitude of misconceptions that I might have not discussed and that also play a prime position in marginalizing feminism and women, I wish these few myths that have been debunked can assist or offer perception to people who have been harassed or felt attacked by them.

For those people who are nevertheless hiding and cautious to publicly embody their feminist beliefs due to the stigma related to the motion, it`s okay. Be pleased with your zeal for equality and change. Never let the lack of knowledge. of others dilute your passion for feminism. Never stop learning about feminism so that you can talk about it shrewdly wherever and whenever you find yourself.

CHAPTER SIX:

THE FIGHT FOR GENDER EQUALITY

Some say that we're a long way from reaching gender equality while others say we are at the leading edge of the fight. We need progress at all levels not limited to:

1. Equal representation and participation

Feminists seek equal representation and participation in social, economic and political roles. Girls and women around the world are already achieving high caliber feats. This is more a reason we need to do away with the gender and age discrimination that threatens their potential. Women's under representation in management roles, significantly in company boardrooms and governmental institutions, constitutes a problem. This under representation hinders the progress of gender equality.

2. Education

Accessible and affordable education will bring progress to the society. Education and support for women's dreams would produce financial and economic solutions, protect the environment and improve health for all. Providing training, education, counseling, medical care, and so on will go a long way in breaking gender-based violence cycles.

3. Economic empowerment and independence

The current system and structures are designed in such a way to favor men than women. We need to rewrite these wrongs. We need to devote our time, energy, loans and resources towards empowering women, rather than creating hindrances and making the system less favorable for them. Empowered women also empower other women and this will yield economic growth. Every woman needs to feel valued.

CHAPTER SEVEN:

EMPOWERING WOMEN AND GIRLS

Empowering girls and women is integral in shaping our future and it has massive advantages for the society. You are an independent, unbiased woman. Fulfill your dreams and ambitions. You have the potential to create the life that you want and you have to inspire other girls and women around you to do the same. Here are a few qualities you'll find useful along the way:

1) Confidence in yourself and your abilities

Never doubt yourself and your abilities. We are competent of far more than we give ourselves credit for. Follow your dreams, not even the sky is your limit.

2) Taking risks

The greatest benefits come from rising from your comfort zone and taking risks. Nothing grows in the comfort zone because you'll be too relaxed to do anything.

3) Be an example

Don't look down on yourself. Set an example to people, especially girls and women around you by what you do. There is no other way to raise fierce, independent girls and women than to be one yourself. Teach them goal-setting and goal-getting, determination and that hard work pays off.

4) Master emotional intelligence

Keep your emotions in check. It's OK to feel sad or anxious sometimes but you must always bounce back, you must always elevate your mood.

5) Be there for "your women" when they need you

Even fierce, independent women need a support system to be at their very best. Show them that you love them, believe in them, and that they don't need to reach a certain criteria for you to love and support them unconditionally. When they flop, comfort them and be there for them.

CHAPTER EIGHT:

IMPORTANCE OF FEMINISM TODAY

WHY IS FEMINISM VITAL IN TODAY`S WORLD?

There are a lot of examples you could refer to in relation to opportunities to show that women and girls are not equal to men and boys in our societies, and the negative impact of this is taking its toll on all of us.

Feminism is important today to close the gender pay and dream gaps, improve health conditions and provide access to education for women all around the world

Empowering women and accomplishing gender equality has massive advantages for the society as a whole. Reduction in poverty, instability, insecurity and gender-based violence; increased innovation, productivity, positive changes in the community and economic growth, etc are some of the benefits that will birthed in the society when gender equality is achieved. Indeed, we will live in a more inclusive and prosperous world if gender equality strives in all nook and cranny.

WHY WE STILL NEED FEMINISM

The standard of feminism, which promotes gender equality, has transformed drastically over time. Feminism continues to be integral today as it ever was, in spite of the incredible achievements in the past. The present day feminism highlights the achievements, obstacles and fight for gender equality.

Where would women be without past feminist actions that have been set in place? Perhaps with worse social and employment opportunities than we have today. This is why feminism is vital today. We've come a long way but we've still got a lot to do. A great deal of work remains though progress has been made in favor of gender equality.

We still need feminism to put an end to the gender pay gap. A lot of the gender pay gap depends on education. There has been advancement in access to education to the female gender, however more is required if we need to close the gender pay gap.

We still need feminism to close the dream gap. Women and girls today still see themselves as being inferior to men and boys.

We still need feminism today because women are still denied leadership and political positions in the society.

We still need feminism today so that women can have an equal chance at success as men.

We still need feminism today because it stands for solidarity, ingenuity and love – values which patriarchy has diminished one way or the other in the name of being tough.

Gender discrimination does not only limit careers but also ruins lives in the most unfair and inhumane ways. We still need feminism today to recognize and protect women from sexual abuse, assault and domestic violence.

Feminism not only fights against the inequality in the society, but also the voices that tell us that feminism is no longer necessary, that it no longer has a place in today's world. Let's spread the word about feminism.

Feminism is not all about women. It advocates for a society that does not relate any ability, activity or clothes with any gender.

Understanding what feminism truly involves is crucial; feminism involves one to stand up to freely choose, and to experience freedom. Feminism does not imply that women have to be incapable. It boils down to the rights each person has.

We can create a society that is fair and equitable for individuals of all genders by embracing an inclusive mindset. We still need feminism to create a promising future.

CHAPTER NINE:

IMPACTS OF FEMINISM IN MODERN SOCIETY

WHAT HAS FEMINISM ACHIEVED SO FAR?

Generations of toil, hard work and sacrifice have produced success in addressing gender inequality, with progress in women's fundamental rights in relation to education, employment possibilities, health care, women's suffrage, equitable pay, political roles and so on.

When women and girls have the materials and opportunities they need to excel, it's a win for everyone, everywhere. In spite of the progress towards gender equality, though slow and uneven, inequality still continues.

HAS FEMINISM WON ANYWHERE?

No society has definitely reached equality totally, even countries in which feminists have supposedly won. Even in locations in which tremendous progress were made, feminism is still far from what it is supposed to be,

Feminism has had tremendous effects on society, transforming and improving the lives of girls and women all over the world. Feminism has challenged social discrimination and addressed inequity, oppression and all the issues that have marginalized women's well-being. It's been a difficult road.

Feminism resists manipulation, ill-treatment and abuse based on gender and sexuality. It strives to accomplish social justice.

SETBACKS IN FEMINISM

Feminism has gone through numerous setbacks over the years such as internal conflict, societal resistance to feminist movements, hostility, violence, criticisms, misconceptions to undermine the feminist movement, etc.

GENDER ROLES

Men and women are physically and physiologically different. We build our personalities and strive to be successful professionally and socially. Our gender roles which traditionally described us are being demolished day by day.

We have long lived in a patriarchal system where men have had more rights and opportunities to develop themselves. From historic times, women had been constrained to cooking, cleansing and child upbringing.

If a woman worked outside the house, it was in a minor role.

In the last century, gender roles have started to change.

The stability of emotional fairness in relationships had shifted too and parental roles are shared by men and women.

The best way to co-exist in the society is to encourage peaceful communication among the genders. We are all sharing identities and roles at different spheres of life. We must assist, support and hear each other out. We need to stop competing for which gender is more superior.

CHAPTER TEN

MISOGYNY

Misogyny is hatred of, contempt for, or violence against women. Misogyny is a monster that keeps women at a disadvantage in society.

These are ways in which we can address misogyny today:

- ✧ Acknowledge it exists.

- ✧ Confront it in your personal life.

- ✧ Challenge others after they showcase misogyny. We need to stand up against injustices when we encounter them.

- ✧ Promote gender equality through awareness, advocacy and support for the rights of women and girls.

- ✧ Support organizations that advocate for gender equality.

SEXISM

Sexism is the belief that one gender is more superior than the other. Addressing sexism is one of the goals of feminism. Sexism presents in various forms such as gender pay gap, workplace discrimination, street harassment, representation in offices and other forms of inequalities.

Here are ways to safely and effectively go against sexism and sexist comments wherever you are:

- ✧ Use your words wisely. Desist from statements that propagate misconceptions and stereotypes about gender.

- ✧ Use humor intelligently. Don't respond to a sexist joke with a laugh. It means you're OK with it.

- ✧ Educate people and create awareness about gender equality and the impacts of sexism.

- ✧ Support people who have gone through one form of sexism or the other.

NOTES